YOUR KNOWLEDGE HAS VALUE

AF151018

- We will publish your bachelor's and master's thesis, essays and papers

- Your own eBook and book - sold worldwide in all relevant shops

- Earn money with each sale

Upload your text at www.GRIN.com and publish for free

Beat Andreas Schweizer

The Assassination of John F. Kennedy

GRIN Verlag

Bibliografische Information der Deutschen Nationalbibliothek:

Die Deutsche Bibliothek verzeichnet diese Publikation in der Deutschen National-
bibliografie; detaillierte bibliografische Daten sind im Internet über http://dnb.d-
nb.de/ abrufbar.

Imprint:

Copyright © 2006 GRIN Verlag GmbH
Druck und Bindung: Books on Demand GmbH, Norderstedt Germany
ISBN: 978-3-656-36079-7

This book at GRIN:

http://www.grin.com/en/e-book/208313/the-assassination-of-john-f-kennedy

GRIN - Your knowledge has value

Der GRIN Verlag publiziert seit 1998 wissenschaftliche Arbeiten von Studenten, Hochschullehrern und anderen Akademikern als eBook und gedrucktes Buch. Die Verlagswebsite www.grin.com ist die ideale Plattform zur Veröffentlichung von Hausarbeiten, Abschlussarbeiten, wissenschaftlichen Aufsätzen, Dissertationen und Fachbüchern.

Visit us on the internet:

http://www.grin.com/

http://www.facebook.com/grincom

http://www.twitter.com/grin_com

Beat Schweizer

Kantonsschule Romanshorn

Klasse 4Me

Maturaarbeit

The Assassination of John F. Kennedy

Fach: English

Abgabetermin: 14. August 2006

Table of Contents

1 Introduction

John Fitzgerald Kennedy was very popular and much adored during his term of office. The world should not yet know about his real personality. In later years after his death, the truth came out. He was not the faithful husband nor was he in good health. Nevertheless, he is still one of the most popular US Presidents ever. He had not deserved to be assassinated. No one has. Inspired by Oliver Stone's Hollywood movie 'JFK', I wanted to know more about the assassination. Who could be responsible for it? Which motivation could someone have to kill the president of the most powerful nation in the world? I do not intend to find the real murderer, I am not competent for that. Yet, I can try to get a picture of the most important theories and evaluate them. I am as well interested in the consequences of the assassination on the world. I think another interesting question is how the people reacted to the assassination. People who were there, and people who only heard it in the news. Both seem to be concerned.

The most exciting part about the assassination is the ignorance. Although over 40 years passed since then, the Kennedy case, as one of very few of the 20th Century, still remains unsolved.

2 Short Biography of JFK[1]

John Fitzgerald Kennedy was born on Mai 29, 1917 in Brookline (Massachusetts/USA) as the son of a diplomat. Originally his family came from Ireland but moved to the USA. John was the second of nine children. In 1926 they moved to New York. From 1936 to 1940 John F. Kennedy studied political science at the Harvard University. He released his final paper "Why England slept" which became a best-seller. The following year he studied management in California but he broke it off soon. During the last four years of World War II he had been serving in the marine voluntarily. In 1943 he was the commander of the speed boat PT 109. Although his boat has been destroyed by Japans and he was injured, Kennedy could rescue most of the crew and he has been made the hero of the disaster. What many people are not aware of, is that Kennedy often suffered from many diseases throughout his life.

"Returning to Massachusetts after the war, he was elected as a Democrat to the US House of Representatives (1947-53) and the US Senate (1953-61)."[2] In 1953 he got married to Jaqueline Bouvier. They had three children. One of them died shortly after birth. In 1956 Kennedy's book "Profiles in Courage" (Zivilcourage) won the Pulitzer Prize.

"Having failed in his 1956 bid for the Democratic vice-presidential nomination, in 1960 he became the youngest man, and first Catholic, to be elected US President."[2] His rival had been later US President Richard Nixon. John Fitzgerald Kennedy was the 35th President of the United States of America. During his term of office he made effort to establish the same rights for black people as for white people. Another important decision was to change the foreign policy of the Cold War into a policy with lots of compromises to guarantee peace. He made effort to retire from Vietnam and to build up a friendly relationship towards Russia. After his death most of his foreign policy was turned back into the former Cold War policy.

One of the most delicate topics was the Cuba Crisis. In 1959 Fidel Castro's revolution triumphed and became a close partner to the USSR. So Cuban exiles which had been trained by the CIA and militarily supported by the USA made an assault on Fidel Castro's regime but they failed. This was a great political fiasco and for Kennedy a personal defeat, too. Later on, "the Russians placed missiles on Cuba wherefore the political balance of power was in great

---

[1] http://www.hdg.de/lemo/html/biografien/KennedyJohnF/
[2] http://history1900s.about.com/gi/dynamic/offsite.htm?zi=1/XJ&sdn=history1900s&zu=http%3A%2F%2Fwww.biography.com%2Fsearch%2Farticle.jsp%3Faid%3D9362930%26search%3D

danger."[3] As a reaction to that, Kennedy ordered an economical embargo against Cuba and set the Soviets under pressure. Finally the Russians retired from Cuba. Thus the danger of a World War III could be averted. "As a result of the Cuba Crisis the USA and USSR installed the 'hot wire', a direct teleprint line between the governments in America and Russia. Both countries agreed on the nuclear test stop."[4] Kennedy was also interested in the situation in Berlin (East-/West under different regimes). Without Kennedy's effort it would have ended in a disaster. In his last year he travelled to Germany and especially to Berlin, where he had his famous speech: "Ich bin ein Berliner!". The German nation was inspired. The very day before his death he ordered to prepare a new programme against poverty. John Fitzgerald Kennedy was assassinated on November 22, 1963 in Dallas/Texas. A few days later he was buried in Arlington.

Because of his early death he became immediately a myth. Although his affairs with women such as Marilyn Monroe tarnished his image in the minds of some people he is still one of the most adorable men of the 20th Century.

---

[3] Maturaarbeit „John F. Kennedy – Profiles in Courage p.9
[4] Maturaarbeit „John F. Kennedy – Profiles in Courage p.13

3 The Assassination

It was November 22, 1963 when John F. Kennedy was visiting Dallas/Texas. Although many Southerners were against him because he supported the Black Civil Rights Movement, Kennedy got a very friendly welcome.

He just wanted to start his campaign for the next election day there when suddenly three shots were fired and the President got deadly injured. He had only been about thousand days in office. There exist a lot of different theories about the murder of JFK (see Chapter 4). Nevertheless, there are also assured facts of the happenings. And that is what I want to list in chapter 3.1.

Famous Picture of Kennedis Lincoln on November 22, 1963[5]

3.1   Chronology of the Assassination

Friday, November 22, 1963

11.38h: The Air Force One lands in Dallas. The motorcade is being prepared.[6]

---

[5] http://en.wikipedia.org/wiki/Image:JFKmotorcade.jpg
[6] http://www.swissdox.ch/cgi-bin/cqcgi_703_5/@rw_sd_set2_minus.de.env?CQ_SESS...

11.50h: Kennedy takes seat in a black Lincoln Continental. He has ordered to use the car without the bullet-proof top; against the advice of his security agents. His wife is sitting together with Kennedy on the back seat of the car. She is on his left-hand side. The governor of Texas, John Connally, and his wife are sitting on the middle seat. On the front seat are the chauffeur and a Secret Service agent. Kennedy is going to have a speech on the Trade Mart. About 250'000 people are waiting for him.

11.55h: Reportedly, the route is shortly changed so that the motorcade passes the Elm Street instead of staying on the Main Street.[7]

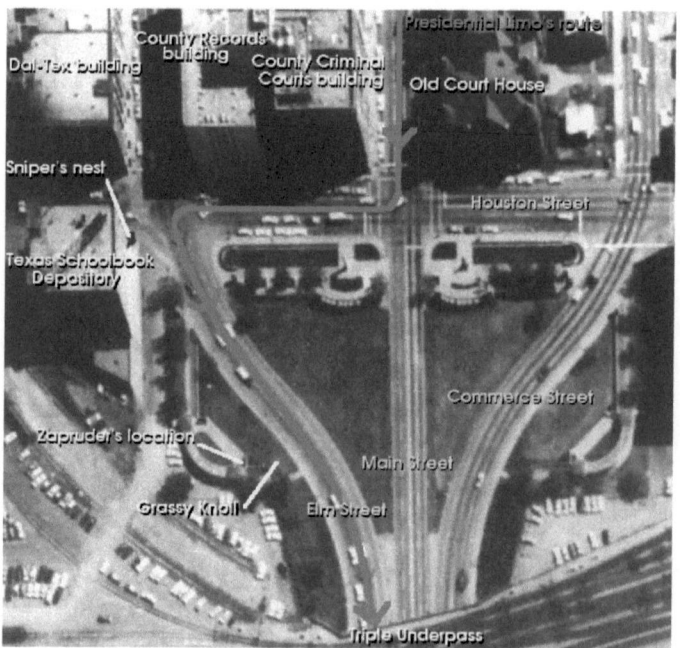

Motorcade route[8]

12.30h: The motorcade is passing the Dealey Plaza (in the middle of the picture) with approximately 11 km/h. About three shots are fired on the President within less than 10 seconds ap-

---

[7] Jim Garrison: *Wer erschoss John F. Kennedy?*, p. 130
[8] http://en.wikipedia.org/wiki/Image:Dealey-plaza-annotated.png

parently from behind. He gets first hurt on his neck. Secret Service agent Clint Hill in the car behind is the only one who reacts brilliantly. He starts running to the Presidential car but another bullet hits Kennedy's head just a touch before Hill reaches the car. Governor Connally is hurt as well. Both together have eight injuries which is a clue that there might have been more than three shots.[9]

"James Tague, a spectator and witness to the assassination, also received a minor wound to his right cheek while standing 270 feet (82 meters) in front of where Kennedy was hit, presumably from debris that shot up when a bullet had hit the curb."[10]

12.36h: The limousine reaches the Parkland Memorial Hospital. Jackie Kennedy is under shock. The doctors try to save him. Useless.

13.00: John F. Kennedy is pronounced dead.

13.06h: Police officer Jefferson David Tippit is anonymously shot.

13.10h: Sniper's nest on 6th floor of the Texas School Book Depository is found. The police finds a Mannlicher- Carcano sniper rifle which had been ordered by Lee Harvey Oswald. Reportedly also a Mauser rifle is found, which disappears for ever soon afterwards.[11]

13.50h: The police arrests in a cinema suspicious 24-year-old Lee Harvey Oswald who has obviously killed police officer Tippit. He is blamed to have killed Kennedy and Tippit which he denies vehemently. Oswald is interrogated during twelve hours. No one keeps any records.

Officer J. D. Tippit[12]

[9] http://de.wikipedia.org/wiki/Attentat_auf_John_F_Kennedy
[10] http://en.wikipedia.org/wiki/Jfk_assassination
[11] Jim Garrison: Wer erschoss John F. Kennedy?, p. 126
[12] http://de.wikipedia.org/wiki/Attentat_auf_John_F_Kennedy

14.20h: Kennedy's dead body is moved to the Air Force One to fly to the Bethesda Naval Hospital in Washington for the autopsy. The pathologists are ordered not to examine Kennedy's injury on the neck. After the autopsy all notes are burned and Kennedy's brain disappears, which can never be examined.[13]

14.38h: Vice-President Lyndon B. Johnson is inaugurated as US President on the Air Force One to prevent a national security emergency.

[13] Jim Garrison: *Wer erschoss John F. Kennedy?*, p. 10
[14] http://en.wikipedia.org/wiki/Lyndon_B._Johnson

Sunday, November 24, 1963

11.31h: Lee Harvey Oswald is shot by local Night Club owner Jack Ruby at the police headquarters in front of running cameras as he should be transferred to prison by police officers. Ruby explains, that he did not want Mrs. Kennedy to be confronted with the lawsuit around Oswald.

Monday, November 25, 1963

14.52h: John F. Kennedy is buried on the National Cemetery of Arlington. About a million people say goodbye.

---

[15] http://en.wikipedia.org/wiki/Image:Oswald_shot_by_Ruby_%28Pulitzer%29.jpg

3.2   Eye witness accounts[16]

Bob Jackson:

"We heard the first shot. Then, we heard two more shots closer together...I just looked straight up ahead of me because that is the direction the sound came from, and I saw two black men leaning out of the window of the fifth floor, looking directly up above them. My eyes went on up to the next floor, and there was the rifle. I could see the rifle...part of the stock, and it being drawn in the window...."

Abraham Zapruder:

"There were police running right behind me. Of course, they did not realize yet, I guess, where the shot came from....I did not even remember how I got down from that abutment but there I was, and I was walking back toward my office and screaming: "They killed him! They killed him!" and the people that I met on the way did not even know what happened, and they kept yelling: "What happened? What happened?" It seemed that they had heard a shot but they did not know exactly what had happened as the car sped away, and I kept on just yelling: "They killed him! They killed him!" And finally I got to my office and my secretary -- I told her to call the police or the Secret Service...I just went to my desk and stopped there until the police came, and then we were required to get a place to develop the films. I knew I had something, I figured it might be of some help -- I did not know what."

Roy Truly:

"...everybody was screaming and hollering. Just moments later I saw a young motorcycle policeman run up to the building, up the steps to the entrance of our building. He ran right by me. And he was pushing people out of the way. I believe I caught up with him inside the lob-by of the building, or possibly the front steps. I remember it occurred to me that this man wants on top of the building. He doesn't know the plan of the floor. I ran in with him. As we got in the lobby, almost on the inside of the first floor, this policeman asked me where the

---

[16] http://historynet.com/ah/bl4days/index3.html

stairway is. And I said, "This way." And I ran diagonally across to the northwest corner of the building.

[On the second floor] I saw the officer almost directly in the doorway of the lunchroom facing Lee Harvey Oswald. He was at the front of the lunchroom, not very far inside....When I reached there, the officer had his gun pointing at Oswald....He did not seem to be excited or overly afraid or anything. He might have been a bit startled, like I might have been if somebody confronted me. But I cannot recall any change in expression of any kind on his face. The officer turned this way and said, "This man work here?" And I said, "Yes." Then we left Lee Harvey Oswald immediately and continued to run up the stairways."

Jacqueline Kennedy:
"I was looking...to the left, and I heard these terrible noises. And my husband never made any sound. So I turned to the right. And all I remember is seeing my husband, he had this sort of quizzical look on his face, and his hand was up, it must have been his left hand. And just as I turned and looked at him, I could see a piece of his skull and I remember it was flesh colored. I remember thinking he just looked as if he had a slight headache. And I just remember seeing that. No blood or anything. And then he sort of...put his hand to his forehead and fell in my lap. And then I just remember falling on him and saying, "Oh, no, no, no!" I mean: "Oh, my God! They have shot my husband!" And "I love you, Jack!" I remember I was shouting. And just being down in the car with his head in my lap. And it just seemed an eternity.

You know, then, there were pictures later on of me climbing out the back. But I don't remember that at all."

Julia Ann Mercer got into a rush hour on the Elm Street an hour before the assassination. She noticed somebody with a rifle bag heading toward the Grassy Knoll. [17]

S. M. Holland, worker at the nearby railroad station, counted four shots. He heard some bang from the Grassy Knoll and saw a cloud of smoke above the tries there. [17]

William Newman, tracer from Dallas, was observing the parade with his family as the shots were fired. First he thought it was a firecracker. When the president was just in front of him he saw his face blowing up and realised that it were shots. He instantaneously laid on the ground to protect his children. He described the sounds coming from behind; from the Grassy Knoll. [18]

3.3 Reactions to the Assassination in Switzerland[19]

"The first hour after the shooting, before Kennedy's death was announced, was a time of great confusion. As it took place during the Cold War, some people at first wondered if the shooting were not part of a larger attack upon the USA, and there was concern about Vice-President Johnson's safety. People began to huddle around radios and TVs for the latest bulletins.

The news of Kennedy's death by assassination shocked the world. In cities around the world, people wept openly. People clustered in department stores to catch TV coverage, and others prayed. Motor traffic in some areas came to a halt as the news of Kennedy's death spread literally from car to car. Most schools across the USA and Canada dismissed students early. All three TV networks cancelled regular programs scheduled for the next three days in order to provide non-stop news coverage of the assassination. The television coverage of the assassination was the longest uninterrupted news coverage of one event until the terrorist attacks on the World Trade Center and the Pentagon.
Memorial services for Kennedy were held worldwide. The US Government declared a day of national mourning and sorrow for the day of his state funeral, Monday, November 25. Many other countries did the same."[20]

---

[17] Jim Garrison: *Wer erschoss John F. Kennedy?*, p. 31- 33
[18] Jim Garrison: *Wer erschoss John F. Kennedy?*, p. 31- 33
[19] All quotations are translated from German into English by Beat Schweizer
[20] http://en.wikipedia.org/wiki/Jfk_assassination

Even in Switzerland the people were shocked. Kennedy had been one of the most popular US-Presidents ever and was well known for his efforts for peace. For some people the tragedy was almost the end of their hope for a better world.

3.3.1 Statements in newspapers[21]

Rosa Brönnimann, Meiringen

"It was horrible! We all cried. At that time I was living at the Längenberg and read the news in the newspaper. Kennedy was so popular and friendly. It was a really sad day."

Ortwin Kohler, Meiringen

"At that time I was a student in Bern and heard the news in the radio. We all were totally shocked and we wondered again and again: "How could that happen?". We were deeply shocked, actually more than on September 11. It was incredible!"

Heinz Brunner, Interlaken

"Then I was 12 years old and saw it on TV. At that time it was shocking that someone could be shot in the open street. Today we are already nearly accustomed to that."

Erika Zangger, Brienz

"It was terrible. We could not believe what had happened. I had admired Kennedy and could not get for a long time that he was dead. The assassination has preoccupied us until today."

Albert Stäheli, Brienz

"It was a very sad experience. Especially due to his confession towards the population of Berlin, which was suffering much from the building up of the Iron Curtain. Except Jimmy Carter the USA never had such a person on whom hopes are pinned like JFK again."

---

[21] http://www.swissdox.ch/cgi-bin/cqcgi_703_5/@rw_sd_set2_minus.de.env?CQ_SESS...
Survey by Susanna Michel on the occasion of the 40th day of JFK's death on November 22, 2003

3.3.2 Personal reactions

I have spoken to some persons about how they had experienced the assassination of JFK.

-Do you remember the day on which John Fitzgerald Kennedy was assassinated?

Brigitte Roman, 33 years of age at that time:
"I cannot remember the day. We heard it in the radio and read it in the newspapers because we did not have a TV at that time. We were bewildered. We could not really believe that something like that had be possible to happen. He was such a perky president. Certainly also because he was catholic. We thought of a plot as soon as Oswald was shot himself. At that time nobody thought that something like that could ever happen. It reminds me on the failed assassination of pope John Paul II."

Elisabeth Schweizer, 32 years of age at that time:
"I cannot remember well anymore. We were concerned. He was so well-known, liked and popular. But in the end we did not have much to do with America, it was too far away."

Richard Schweizer:
"I remember well. I was about 31 years old. I was driving home with the car when I suddenly heard the news in the car radio. It was about 18.00 or 18.30, something like that. As I arrived at home, I also saw the tragedy on TV. We already had a TV at that time. We were totally shocked! How could such a nutter shoot the US President out of the sky? Kennedy was very popular. The whole world was astonished that someone could kill him in the open car. Nowadays there is actually much more going on in this world of course. Yet, at that time really the whole world was filled with mourning. The Kennedy family was a huge Clan. They had to sustain many heavy strokes of fait during all the time, although they had a very huge sum of money. For example Robert Kennedy was then assassinated, too. This shows that you cannot always handle anything with money."

Jolanda Egloff:

"Yes, I remember that day as if it were yesterday, although I was only eight years old at that time. We were living in Lucerne. I was in school, we had religious education. Then, the mistress entered the classroom and told us about Kennedy being assassinated. I seriously hoped that it was the other Kennedy, Robert and not John. Then we prayed for him all together and sang songs as well. It was very impressive! After school I ran home and found out that it was John. This day has been bothering me for a very long time. In fact, it was the main topic of conversation. Some days after this had happened we watched his funeral. As we were one the first families which had already a TV, almost the whole neighbourhood joined us. There was a huge consternation. Everyone had hoped Kennedy would finally change America. We lived in a permanent fear of the hot topics such as the racial segregation, Vietnam and the Cold War with Russia. We feared a third world war. But of course I did not really get that at the age of eight.

We were convinced of a governmental plot against Kennedy from the very beginning. Kennedy had opened the country too much and too quickly. It were the right wings, Ku Klux-Clan, CIA. Oswald was just a patsy, he was abused. It seemed already strange as he was arrested so quickly. I would always strictly refuse the theory of a crazy loner."

-Has that day influenced your life?

Brigitte Roman:

"No, it has not. Certainly, we spoke for a long time about it yet. Particularly the assassination of Robert Kennedy refreshed the tragedy. But by and by we accepted the fact."

Richard Schweizer:

"I noticed the death of the president of the most powerful nation as a very tragically misery. I was then occupied by other, more important problems. I was already blessed with a family and children and had to run a business. Over the years I could put away that sad day. It was about 1978 when I visited Dallas. I was shown a film about the assassination which was so impressive, that I thought it was real. It appeared like lively reliving it. Such a good film can only be made by the Americans! Whenever I was about to rehear something about the assassination of Kennedy it bothered me anew."

Jolanda Egloff:
"I have been being concerned for a long time. We all were filled with anxiety for the international stability. As I have already said, I had not really gotten the political aspects of the assassination. I was more anxious about the children, that they have enough money to eat. I did not know about the richness of the Kennedys at that time. I always admired Kennedy as a perfect person. Later on I found out that Kennedy had not been that man I had believed him to be. And suddenly Robert Kennedy was assassinated as well. He was always the better politician of them. He was the mover behind John. This was another shock for me. Over the years I accepted the situation. I had to; there is nothing else for it!"

4   Theories

The mystery around the assassination of John F. Kennedy could not be solved till this day. Over the years many people have advanced a huge amount of different theories about the assassination so that it is very difficult to figure out whom to believe. In this chapter I would like to examine the most likely and established theories more closely.

4.1   Warren Commission[22]

The Warren Commission was established by president Lyndon B. Johnson on November 29, 1963 to determine the circumstances of the assassination. A more important reason was to calm the sentiments of the population which was worried by the many conspiracy theories. Johnson pressed the investigation to be finished very quickly. The Commission therefore worked under high pressure.

It was named after its chairman Earl Warren. The members were Senator John Sherman Cooper (Republican), Allen Welsh Dulles (former CIA-Director), Gerald Ford (Republican, later US-President), Hale Boggs (Democrat), Senator Richard B. Russell (Democrat) and John J. McCloy (former president of the World Bank).

Only one year later the Commission came to the conclusion that it must have been a 'one man operation'. The Commission reported that it could not find any persuasive evidence of a conspiracy and that Lee Harvey Oswald was the only assassin and that Jack Ruby acted alone in the murder of Oswald as well. according to the Commission, Oswald had no motive. He was just a psychopath. The Warren Report which contains approximately 900 pages was published. As a result of the investigation over 600 witnesses were consulted and about 3000 pieces of evidence were secured.

According to the Commission's theory, Lee Harvey Oswald started his work at the Texas School Book Depository (TSBD) at 8.00 a.m. He has been working there for a few weeks. He shall have fired the deadly shots from the 6th floor of the TSBD with the Carcano rifle. One shot hits Kennedy's head (final shot), one shot missed him totally and one bullet caused the other seven injuries of Kennedy and Connally (Magic Bullet Theory). Oswald attracted attention as he left the TSBD three minutes after the assassination. Soon afterwards the police broadcast the description of a suspicious person, namely Oswald, based on the statement of a witness who had seen him at a window of the TSBD. Oswald took the bus and later on a taxi. He arrived at 13.00 p.m. at his apartment where he changed clothes and took his revolver. This was reported by his landlady. At 13.05 p.m. Oswald was seen at a nearby bus station. At 13.15 p.m. when police officer J. D. Tippit tried to arrest Oswald, he shot Tippit with four shots. About a dozen witnesses can affirm it. Thereon Oswald entered the 'Texas Theatre' cinema without paying. Therefore the cashier called the police who arrested Lee Harvey Oswald at 13.50 p.m. Two days later, Oswald is shot by Jack Ruby at the police station. Ruby justified himself with the explanation that he wanted to save Mrs. Kennedy from the trial of her husband's murderer and that he took revenge for the death of his president.

4.1.1 Pro[23]

A Carcano rifle and three bullet casings were found on the 6th floor of the TSBD. The rifle had been ordered by Lee Harvey Oswald. As the assassination took place, Oswald was staying in that building and was not seen at the precise point in time. Oswald's fingerprints were found in the room where the rifle was hidden and on the rifle itself, too.

With a nitrate test could be proved that Oswald had traces of nitrate on his hands. This means either that he had fired a weapon in the last 24 hours when the assassination had taken place or that the traces came from his work in the depot.[24]

Furthermore Oswald was known as a crazy loner. He had been distributing pro-Castro flyers and he had been the president of the 'Fair Play for Cuba Committee'. With this activities it seems that Oswald had somehow a political motive to kill the president. It also exists a very charging photo of Oswald which shows him with the rifle and a communistic newspaper.

---

[22] http://de.wikipedia.org/wiki/Attentat_auf_John_F._Kennedy /
http://en.wikipedia.org/wiki/Lee_Harvey_Oswald#Oswald.27s_flight_and_the_murder_of_Officer_J._D._Tippit
[23] Zellweger, Kim: Maturaarbeit "Das Attentat auf John F. Kennedy" p. 3

[24] http://de.wikipedia.org/wiki/Attentat_auf_John_F._Kennedy

Oswald with the Carcano rifle and The Daily Worker[25]

Jack Ruby was a very emotional person who could easily lose his temper. All his friends believed him not to be part of a conspiracy. If he was a part of a plot, someone would have had to silence Ruby, and someone other to silence Ruby's murderer and so on.

4.1.2 Contra

Some people claim that there were not any fingerprints on the rifle until Oswald died. This would mean that the fingerprints were added belatedly; consequently faked. Actually it is unlikely that the Carcano had been fired at all. The rifle was rather imprecise, in a bad state and the sight was badly fixed. Nevertheless, later investigations came to the conclusion that the Carcano rifle had been definitely fired. Oswald's skills as a sniper were reportedly average. The best FBI snipers were not able to iterate Oswald's accomplishment. Therefore it is almost impossible that he fired the three shots with that rifle within ca. 5.6 seconds, as first assumed. In fact, he had stupidly over 8s time to do so which is quite enough. However, the three bullet casings of the Carcano rifle were artificially laid on the ground. One close after the other.

Mostly the first shot is the best but in this case the last shot was the deadly one. This argues for another sniper. Although in the meantime new tape material was found and the analysis showed that at least four shots had been fired from at least two different directions, this material is worthless to prove anything (See chapter 4.5).[26]

---

[25] http://icky.de/index2.htm
[26] http://icky.de/index2.htm

Connally and Kennedy had too many injuries than could be caused by three shots. The Single Bullet Theory is very improbable.

The "magic" or single bullet theory.

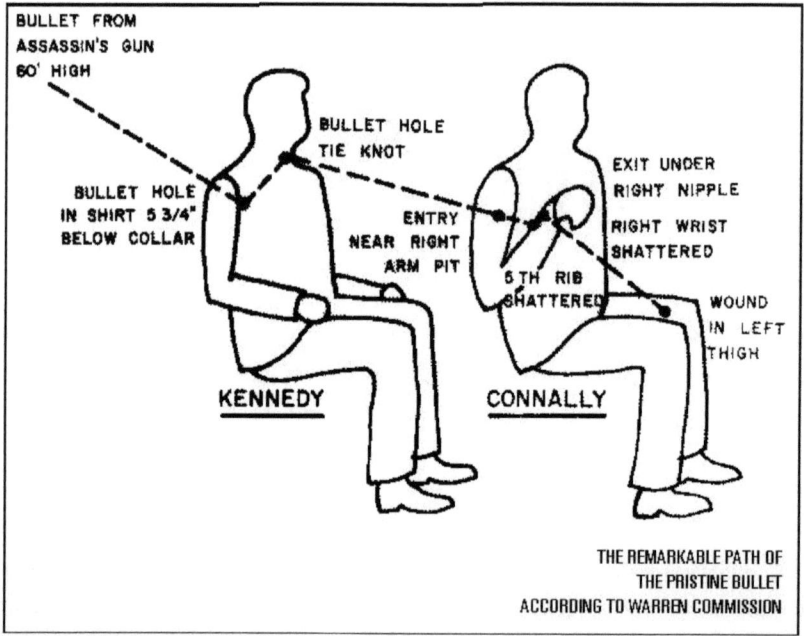

Another diagram of the single bullet theory.

Source: HIGH TREASON

The Magic Bullet Theory[27]

Furthermore Oswald was seen calmly drinking a coke at the 2nd floor of the TSBD only two minutes after the happenings (see eye witness account of Roy Truly). One cannot hide a rifle, run four floor downwards and calmly drink a coke within that time.[28]

Concerning the photo of Oswald with his rifle, a precise analysis showed that the photo is faked. His face doesn't exactly go with the body and the neck.[29] Yet, the latest analyses showed that the photo was never faked.

---

[27] http://icky.de/index2.htm
[28] Jim Garrison: *Wer erschoss John F. Kennedy?*, p.126

All in all the Warren Commission did a rather unsatisfying work, probably because they had too less time. This must be the reason why many people did not accept this theory from the very first and why there are so many conspiracy theories.

4.2 Jim Garrison

Jim Garrison[30]

Jim Garrison was District Attorney of New Orleans from 1962 to 1973. When new hints guided to New Orleans in 1966 he felt responsible to start an investigation on the JFK assassination. Thereon he selected his team and started work. After many years of investigation he came to the conclusion that it must have given a conspiracy.

At the beginning he thought that the Warren Commission had completely solved the crime and believed in the official theory of Oswald as a crazy loner. But as soon as he had studied the Warren Report he recognised that there was much sloppiness. Many evidences had disappeared under mysterious circumstances or had been manipulated. He charged especially the FBI for destroying evidences. Furthermore he discovered too many discrepancies and that a number of eye witnesses who would have led to another conclusion had been ignored by the Warren Commission.[31] It was rather strange that the FBI had completed its investigation with

---

[29] Jim Garrison: *Wer erschoss John F. Kennedy?*, p. 97
[30] http://en.wikipedia.org/wiki/Jim_Garrison
[31] Jim Garrison: *Wer erschoss John F. Kennedy?*, p.8

the accusation of Oswald already after several weeks. Garrison came to the conclusion that Oswald had not shot officer J.D. Tippit. The FBI-laboratory confirmed the four bullets found were different to Oswald's revolver. There had been stuck two different types of bullets in Tippit's body which means that probably two shooters had killed him. The homicide squad manipulated the evidence by adding belatedly a bullet of Oswald's revolver.[32]

As a next step Garrison searched for information relating Oswald to New Orleans. Several indices argued for Oswald being a CIA agent. While Oswald had been in the army, he had had to do exams in Russian. After serving to the army Oswald had travelled to the USSR where he had got to know his wife. Back from Russia he had moved to Dallas where his new family had been supported by anti-Communists. Garrison assumed that Oswald had been sent to the Soviet Union by the CIA to do undercover work. While he had been there different persons had appeared under the name of Oswald in the USA.

By 1963 Oswald had moved to New Orleans where he then had been distributing pro-Castro flyers. Moreover Garrison found out that Oswald had been in touch with Guy Banister, a private detective from New Orleans and former FBI agent, David Ferrie, a pilot, and Clay Shaw, a respectable businessman and former CIA agent. Banister's bureau was surrounded by the FBI and CIA quarters. Many anti-Castro Cuban exiles consorted there. It seems quite weird that a later assassin is staying in that milieu. Garrison discovered their relations to the intelligence services. They had been involved in the CIA program of recruiting Cubans and equipping them with weapons to overthrow Fidel Castro.

Meanwhile Garrison was convinced that the responsible persons were to find in the rows of the CIA. Oswald was only made the scapegoat, as he said himself after being arrested: "I did not shoot anyone. Theyare taking me in because of the fact that I lived in the Soviet Union. I am just a patsy!"

Garrison claimed that the areal' Oswald had not been a Communist and that he had not shot at all. The CIA should have manipulated Oswald so that he appeared in public as a crazy loner which suited the official theory. Therefore the false Oswalds during his absence.[33]

It seems as if the CIA would have had a motiv to kill John F. Kennedy. The Bay of Pigs Invasion in 1961 was an important CIA operation executed by Cuban exiles. Although Kennedy

---

[32] Jim Garrison: *Wer erschoss John F. Kennedy?*, p. 257/258

[33] Jim Garrison: *Wer erschoss John F. Kennedy?*, p.81

had ordered the invasion he prohibited to send air support so that the whole operation became a great fiasco. The CIA wanted to continue the Cold War and to destroy every sort of Communism by any means. Although Kennedy promised to follow a strict anti-Communism foreign policy before he was elected president, he felt forced to change his mind later on (see Chapter 2). He closed all official CIA training camps for the Cuban exiles and fired CIA director Allen Dulles, who was a member of the Warren Commission later on, and his deputy director, too.[34] Thereby Kennedy had definitely powerful enemies. After Kennedy's death, the US-Government followed again the line of the Cold War, thanks to president Johnson. Thus Garrison named the assassination a fully succeeded coup d'état.

Jim Garrison was never that interested in the question 'Who had actually killed Kennedy?'. He wanted rather to know who was standing behind the assassination, who was responsible for it. For being able to kill the president of the United States and to hush up all evidences of a plot afterwards, help of all organisations of security is needed. Most probably Cold Warriors from the CIA, FBI, Secret Service, Dallas Police and the Warren Commission were involved in the Kennedy conspiracy. Important to know is that never the whole organisation is responsible but only some individuals, mostly from the higher levels.

In 1967, Garrison arrested Clay Shaw and accused him of the participation on the plot to kill Kennedy, which Shaw always denied. Until the lawsuit about two years passed. In the meantime CIA agents, as Garrison later will find out, joined Garrison's crew to infiltrate and sabotage his works.[35] Unfortunately, Garrison's main witness David Ferrie died under mysterious circumstances. Garrison supposed he was murdered. This made the case for Garrison very difficult to win. In 1969 the lawsuit took place. The 'Zapruder Film' – this is an amateur film recorded by Abraham Zapruder (see Chapter 3.2) and shows Kennedy being shot - was shown in public for the first time. Shaw was found not guilty after only 45min because of too less evidences. Nevertheless the court had to admit that the assassination of John F. Kennedy must have been based on a conspiracy.

4.2.1 Pro

Reportedly the motorcade route was changed in the last second so that the Presidential Car passed the Elm Street. Who could better achieve this than people from the government?

---

[34] Jim Garrison: *Wer erschoss John F. Kennedy?*, p. 131/132
[35] Jim Garrison: *Wer erschoss John F. Kennedy?*, p. 227

Although Oswald was being interrogated during twelve hours, no one kept any records. Actually this is a routine and can not be forgotten accidentally. This speaks for the involvement of FBI agents who did the interrogation. In the course of the official Warren Commission investigation several evidences and files disappeared. The autopsy was badly done. The reason: The military pathologists argued about who would make the autopsy. In the end they did it all together. There was not any official medicolegal expert with experience in gunshot wounds and they did not even make a report.[36] Why would people do so if Oswald was the lone gunman?

During his investigations, Jim Garrison was constrained. Files disappeared, the mass media made him a hard life and his work was sabotaged by his own assistants. Finally he detected them to be CIA agents. The only reason for this actions would be a CIA involvement in the assassination.

The FBI was warned about the assassination five days before. Although the FBI-Headquarter sent telegrams to every bureau, they did not react.[37]

A police log and tape recordings show that this is true. William Somersett, an informant of the Miami Police Department recorded secretly a dialogue with the wealthy businessman Joseph Milteer on November 5, 1963. Milteer: "Kennedy is a dead man!". On the question how the assassination would go on, he replied: "From a block of offices...with a precision rifle. It is no match to bring the weapon in individual parts into the building." Milteer did not tell where he had gotten the information from. He just said there was a huge amount of money in the pie. In another tape recording from November 23, 1963, one day after the assassination, Milteer said: "Lee Harvey Oswald won't say anything and nobody needn't worry." The next day, Oswald was dead.[38]

Further, over 50 witnesses affirmed having heard shots from the 'Grassy Knoll'. Dr. Nichols, expert in pathology, came to the conclusion that it was a crossfire after analysing the 'Zapruder Film' and a number of photos. Two snipers had shot from behind from different directions before the final shot had hit Kennedy from the front.[39]

---

[36] Zellweger, Kim: *Maturaarbeit "Das Attentat auf John F. Kennedy",* 2003 p. 15 Quotation of Dr. Markwalder, forensic doctor in St. Gallen

[37] Jim Garrison: *Wer erschoss John F. Kennedy?,* p. 282
[38] Blick; November 24, 1994
[39] Jim Garrison: *Wer erschoss John F. Kennedy?,* p. 306

There were many persons in circles of the CIA who did not agree with Kennedy's policy. They had the power to murder him and to hush up the trails to them.

4.2.2   Contra

Indeed the *Dallas Morning News* showed no turn to Elm Street in its map of the parade route, but because the map was too small. Garrison claimed that it filled almost the whole front side. That is not true. Another newspaper, the *Dallas Times-Herald* showed the Elm Street in its map. And both newspapers had published a printed description of the parade route already on November 19, 1963; with a turn to Elm Street. So there was no change of the parade route.[40]

The 'Zapruder Film' does neither prove if there were several assassins nor wherefrom the final shot was fired. There is no physical reaction of the head to the shot. That means, when a headshot enters from the front, the head can move backwards or forwards, depending on which nerves are hit. More interesting is the blood. It splashed forward, which is the case when the bullet hits from behind.

Excerpt from the 'Zapruder Film', which shows the final shot[41]

In addition, the film shows only the last two shots. This gives Oswald not 5.6s but over 8s time to fire.[42]

About twelve witnesses recognised Oswald as the man who killed officer Tippit.

Some people claim that Garrison was a liar who was obsessed of gaining publicity. He used witnesses with lack of credibility. Garrison claimed some discoveries of other people to be his own.[43] While Garrison was investigating, many inconsistencies arose. He just overlooked them, as files of Garrison, opened in 1995, reveal. Garrison is blamed for having no case

---

[40] http://mcadams.posc.mu.edu/route.htm
[41] http://icky.de/index2.htm
[42] Der Bund; 15.11.2003

against Shaw. He damaged the image of an 'innocent' businessman. This was a travesty of justice.[44]

The Garrison theory is a very spectacular one, but in its entirety of evidences one of the most substantiated and convincingly theories. The reason why it is not the official one is, that it is too challenging and contradicts to the American myth of a law-abiding country.[45] This theory would seriously call the US government and it's Constitution into question. The opinions about Jim Garrison go apart. Was he a hero and detected the true story but bungled the chance to establish it in court, or was he just a selfish liar, who wanted to attract attention!? In the end, Earling Carothers Garrison (November 20, 1921 - October 21, 1992) remains still a controversial figure.

---

[43] http://mcadams.posc.mu.edu/jimlie.htm
[44] http://www.posner.com/articles/garrison.htm
[45] Jim Garrison: *Wer erschoss John F. Kennedy?,* p. 378 Epilogue by Carl Oglesby

4.3   Fidel Castro[46]

Fidel Castro[47]

If we started from a conspiracy, there would be several possible persons behind, who did not commit the act but who are rather responsible for it. Jim Garrison is convinced of the guilty of the CIA and other national facilities. Other people suspect Fidel Castro of the murder of J. F. Kennedy. The conflict between the US-government and Castro is well known. The CIA tried to assassin Castro several times. Therefore Castro would have had a motive to kill the US-leader to take revenge for that. The United States government has never investigated the Cuban role any further, due to the volatile relations between the USA and Cuba. Lyndon B. Johnson believed, that if the American public were to know Cuba was responsible for the death of Kennedy, they would demand an invasion of Cuba and this would have ended in a nuclear war. Johnson himself was personally convinced that it was Castro.

In 2006, after five years of work, the documentary film 'Rendezvous with Death' was released by the ARD. The film is named after Kennedy's favourite poem:

But I've a rendezvous with Death
At midnight in some flaming town,
When spring trips north again this year,
And I to my pledged word am true,
I shall not fail that rendezvous
(from 'Rendezvous with Death', by Alan Seeger)[48]

---

[46] Tages-Anzeiger, 06.01.2006
[47] http://files.blog-city.com/files/A05/141484/p/f/young_castro_2.jpg
[48] http://www.wdr.de/tv/dokumentation/rendezvous_mit_dem_tod.phtml

They have found new hints guiding to Fidel Castro. The film is based on the statements of several witnesses; one of them is Oscar Marino, who was a member of the Cuban Foreign Secret Service 'G-2' and confirmed that they were responsible for the assassination. Film director Huismann looked for information about Oswald's six-day long stay in Mexico-City in September 1963. During that time, Oswald had had an intensive relationship to the Cuban embassy. The theory says that the Cuban engaged Oswald for killing Kennedy after being recommended by the KGB. "In return, the Cuban government reportedly paid Oswald the sum of $6,500 (with inflation, $40,000 in 2006)."[49] Oswald was probably the only shooter but the executing part of a conspiracy.

Another witness is former FBI investigator Laurence Keenan who travelled to Mexico-City after the assassination to find information about Oswald's stay there. He found a hot trace. But just three days later, FBI director Edgar Hoover ordered him back to Washington immediately, which burdened him all life long.

One might wonder how such a tiny nation like Cuba can handle such a huge event like the JFK assassination. Thereon the answer of a Cuban officer of high rank: "For that very reason why nobody doesn't believe us capable of it, we are going to try it."

4.3.1 Pro

As a matter of fact, there was a crisis between the USA and Cuba, caused by the Bay of Pigs Invasion. This escalated in the Cuba Crisis in 1962. This could have brought Castro to a revenge strike. The fear from a military escalation could have led the investigators not to name the true culprit. During the investigation of Huismann, he discovered many evidences which prove that the Cubans were somehow involved in the assassination or that they had at least something to do with Oswald. This were photos, reports from the Cuban Secret Service DFS and tape recordings. The most important prove are the statements of three former G-2 officers who confirm the guilt of Fidel Castro and the Cubans.[50]

Furthermore Oswald distributed the Pro-Castro flyers. This can mean that he was a pro-Castro himself. Yet, when we assume that this was ordered by someone else, for example by the CIA, this means that the CIA wanted to direct the suspicion to Fidel Castro.

---

[49] http://en.wikipedia.org/wiki/Kennedy_assassination_theories#Two_shooters
[50] http://www.wdr.de/tv/dokumentation/rendezvous_mit_dem_tod.phtml

It only makes sense when Castro ordered the flyers to direct the suspicion to himself; nobody thinks that he would be so stupid, which leads to a false interpretation of the flyers. Thereby Castro leads the suspicion away from him.

4.3.2 Contra

Although the relationship between the USA and Cuba was not that good, Kennedy made much effort to establish a friendly relationship towards Cuba in his last months of presidency. This is known from new documents published in 2003.[51] Kennedy refused to attack Cuba and could stop the Cuban Crisis within twelve days. Why should Castro want L. B. Johnson to substitute Kennedy, to substitute the Kennedy's peace policy for Johnson's Cold War policy? And why should he take revenge after the Crisis instead of during? Could he count on the cooperation of the key figures of the Dallas Police, FBI and CIA, which was necessary for the operation? It is quite weird to believe that the Cubans let Oswald distributing Pro-Castro flyers and call him to kill Kennedy afterwards.[52]

In the late 70ies the *House Select Committee on Assassinations*, a new official investigation, asked Castro personally whether he was it or not. He negated with the answer, that this would have been stupid. Otherwise the USA would have had the perfect reason to invade Cuba; what Castro had tried to avoid all the years.

At the end there are no explicit evidences against the Castro theory. It is only a matter of logic. But who has ever said that the world is logical?! Although there are several documents guiding to the Cubans it is no prove for their guilt. At least every document can always be faked! Further, the film does not make clear whether Castro personally authorized the assassination or not. All in all the Castro theory should be taken serious.

---

[51] Tages Anzeiger; 06.01.2006
[52] Jim Garrison: *Wer erschoss John F. Kennedy?*, p. 362/363

4.4 Mafia

There was another official investigation from 1976 to 1979, the *House Select Committee on Assassinations*. It came to the conclusion that the Secret Services systematically suppressed evidences from the Warren Commission, which would have led into a completely different direction. Lee Harvey Oswald was still the assassin who killed Kennedy but he was not the only shooter anymore; someone else had shot from the 'Grassy Knoll' but had failed. Newly Oswald was now officially a part of a greater plot whose backers are not to detect. Most probably the 'organised crime' signs responsible, which means the Mafia.[53] It is said that Jack Ruby had worked for the Mafia. Thence the murder of Oswald was a Mafia request. Kennedy was the only president to try to eradicate the Mafia. In fact some boss-men really hated Kennedy. Therefore the Mafia would have had a motive to kill him.

4.4.1 Pro

Although the Mafia supported Kennedy at the beginning - it got the votes from Illinois in 1960, which made sure that Kennedy could enter the White House and it provided him with women during his first year of presidency - , their relationship turned into a desperate fight with the Department of Justice; Kennedy meant business with the eradication of the Mafia.[54] There are several connections between Jack Ruby and the Mafia. If the murder of Oswald was a Mafia order, it would mean that the Mafia wanted to silence Oswald and to avoid the trial. Which reason could they have for that if they were not connected with the assassination?

4.4.2 Contra

On the other hand, would the Mafia have had the possibility to change the motorcade route shortly before the parade? Could the Mafia order the pathologists not to examine Kennedy's neck injury and to burn the notes of the autopsy? No, the Mafia had not the means to do so. However, the history shows that the Mafia was sometimes a co-operating organisation to the CIA, maybe until now. Examples are the Sicily drive during the Second World War or the war of the CIA against the Cuban Revolution. It was always the CIA, which led the missions,

---

[53] http://de.wikipedia.org/wiki/Attentat_auf_John_F._Kennedy
[54] Jim Garrison: *Wer erschoss John F. Kennedy?*, p. 384

and not the Mafia.[55] Hence it is unlikely that the Mafia was the only responsible organisation in the assassination of John F. Kennedy.

Nevertheless, it is likely that the Mafia acted as a co-operating organisation to the CIA. Probably the snipers were Mafia killers. According to Jim Garrison, practically every governmental machinery was involved in the assassination. So it would be 'impossible' for the Mafia to corrupt and control them. Yet, I wonder whether this is really that impossible!

4.5   Recent findings

The latest cognition shows, that the theory of Oswald acting as a loner is not unlikely anymore. In fact, it is even the most probable one. Newest computer technology allows to make a computer animated reproduction of the assassination on the basis of different amateur films. It could prove that the sound recording from the microphone of a policeman on the bike in the presidential column was worthless. By the means of that recording the *House Select Committee on Assassinations* came to the conclusion of a conspiracy in 1979. Experts had concluded that it four shots were to hear in minimum. This fact was based on an assumption; the policeman had had to be within a certain distance to the presidential car. The animation shows that he was not there where he was supposed to be. In addition, it shows how the Magic Bullet Theory is possible. Actually, the bullet was not magic. Kennedy and Connally were not exactly sitting back-to-back. They were not even at the same height. Moreover, Connally was not sitting straightly but a bit turned.[56]

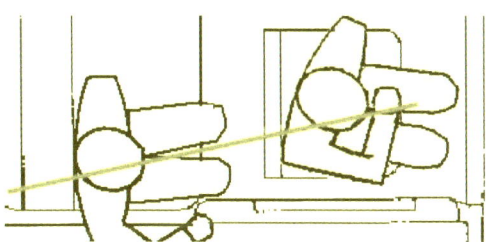

The Bullet is not magic anymore.[57]

---

[55] Jim Garrison: *Wer erschoss John F. Kennedy?*, p. 385
[56] ntv-reportage ‚Die Ermordung John F. Kennedy's'
[57] http://verschwoerungen.info/wiki/John_F._Kennedy

Therefore the bullet flew always straight on and caused the many injuries; without any magical help.

When Gerald Posner, an investigative journalist, wrote his book 'Case Closed'(1993), he came to the conclusion that Oswald had acted alone and shut the file 'Kennedy plot' with it. Impartially he got granular on all the conspiracy theories and could find convincingly arguments against them. He came to the conclusion that Oswald had laid tracks guiding to Cuba and Moscow to arrange a political crisis. In addition, he create his image with the photos of him with the rifle and a communist newspaper to ensure his 'posthumous fame'. Oswald was obsessed of attracting public attention.

Another author, Norman Mailers came independently to the same conclusion in his book 'Oswald's Tale'(1995). He concentrated more on the biography, psyche and motivation of Oswald. "The Oswald that Mailer depicts is a single-minded and vain individual convinced of his own destiny and importance who suffers a series of defeats and frustrations, and kills the President in a desperate search for achievement."[58] The only reason why he killed Kennedy is that he had the chance to influence history from his workplace and to become a significant person of the world. According to Mailers, conspiracy theories only detract from the incomprehensible. Most humang beings can better live with the thought of the monstrosity of a conspiracy instead of the banality of a lone actor.[59]

Both author's books have been established and are generally well respected. Almost every historian to be taken serious has the same opinion.

Finally, there are no evidences neither for a conspiracy nor against. Yet, there is no longer any doubt   about   the   guilt   of   the   crazy   Lee   Harvey   Oswald.

---

[58] http://en.wikipedia.org/wiki/Oswald%27s_Tale
[59] Der Bund; 15.11.2003

5   Consequences of the Assassination on the World

In the end it makes no difference between a conspiracy and a one-man action; people all around the world were shocked and J. F. Kennedy was dead either way. Some people have made profit of the tragedy. At the 6th floor of the TSBD is a museum today. People offer sight seeing tours of the JFK assassination in Dallas together with an introduction in conspiracy theories.

The assassination of John Fitzgerald Kennedy has changed the world. People became aware that a person can be shot on the street in broad daylight. They began to be more careful towards strangers.

From today's view it is very difficult to judge how history would have taken its course if Kennedy had not been assassinated. Perhaps he would have been able to avoid the Vietnam War. "US combat troops were involved in the Vietnam conflict from 1959, but not in large numbers until 1963."[60] In October 1963 Kennedy realised that they were confronted with a situation of which they cannot get out as the winner and took about thousand soldiers back to the USA. Kennedy planned to detail all his troops until the end of the year 1965. Unfortunately, after Kennedy's death his successor Lyndon Baines Johnson sent the thousand soldiers back to Vietnam and by 1968 there were 550'000 US-soldiers inside. In 1968 and 1969 they were being killed by a rate of over 1000 a month. At the end of the Vietnam War in 1975 over 55'000 US soldiers and about one million Vietnamese were slain, among them a very large number of civilian casualties.

In case of a CIA conspiracy it really made profit of the assassination. Under Johnson it retrieved its power in policy. Johnson was a man who corresponded to the CIA's ideas of continuing the war in Vietnam. The reason for the Vietnamese territory's importance must be that a communistic power over the whole Southeast Asian territory would endanger America's position in the pacific ocean and seriously gamble with fundamental security interests of the United States in Far East.[61]

---

[60] http://en.wikipedia.org/wiki/War_of_vietnam
[61] Jim Garrison: *Wer erschoss John F. Kennedy?*, p. 230

John F. Kennedy's death has been a trauma for the American population until now. He represented their dreams and hopes of peace, a better world, generosity and equality as no other president ever would. He attempted to build a better world; in cooperation with all the rest of the world.[62]

Perhaps we would be better off today if Kennedy had not been shot.

Kennedy in his never made speech on November 22, 1963:

"The US Army will never be used on purpose of aggressive ambitions, but will always serve for peace. It will never be used to provoke, it will always be used to support the peaceful settlement of a dispute!"[63]

Perhaps we would not have the problems in Middle East, perhaps we would. Perhaps there were not so many terrorists these days, perhaps there would. In the end nothing else remains than speculations.

---

[62] http://www.3sat.de/3sat.php?http://www.3sat.de/kulturzeit/themen/53102/index.html
[63] http://www.3sat.de/3sat.php?http://www.3sat.de/kulturzeit/themen/53102/index.html
Translated from German

6   Conclusion

Fact is that John Fitzgerald Kennedy was assassinated on November 22, 1963 in Dallas and died. People all around the world were shocked or at least concerned. Who was responsible for it? It has been unknown until this day. Officially Lee Harvey Oswald killed Kennedy. Although many people have disbelieved it, Oswald's guilt is finally assured. Not assured is, whether he was a part of a conspiracy or not. I personally believe in Oswald being a part of a conspiracy of the government, CIA, FBI. Otherwise I could not explain how there exist so many rumours about faked documents, disappeared evidences and corrupted witnesses. Actually, the main problem of the Kennedy case is corruption. We don't know which documents are faked, which pictures are constructed and which facts are false. It is impossible to find the truth with hindsight for someone who had nothing to do with the assassination at that time. He can only read about the happenings, but he can never be sure if it is correct. Finally, all my paper is only an assumption, a thesis. I was told every information by any source and don't know if it is true. That is something I have learnt through my work; you can never be sure about something you have read unless you have investigated yourself. Everyone can write whatever he wants to.

In the end I must admit, that it was hard work for me. The main part was to figure out which facts, which sources to use. There are not many newer historical books about the assassination. Many authors made a thriller out of their inquests, mixed with fiction. In newer time the debate about the murder of Kennedy was displaced to the internet, where it is quite difficult to find useful facts. After reading Garrison's book 'On the trail of the Assassins' I was convinced that this was the truth. Yet, as soon as I found sources which disproved some of it's statements, I realised that it was rather more difficult as I had assumed. Perhaps Garrison was lying, perhaps he did not know it better. Nevertheless, I believe him concerning the guilt of the CIA.

I would especially like to thank Brigitte Roman, Richard and Elisabeth Schweizer and Jolanda Egloff for their disposition of telling me their personal experiences. It was really interesting to listen and helped me a lot for my paper. B. Roman, R. and E. Schweizer are my grandparents, J. Egloff is a friend. I would also like to thank Mrs. Pazeller, who supported me quite well during my work. Although it was a lot of work for me, I have learned much about the happenings and about life in general as well. I am very glad for having chosen this topic.

Bibliography

Burda, Dr. Franz: *John F. Kennedy.* Gedenkband der Bunten Illustrierten. Baden: Burda
   Druck und Verlag

Garrison, Jim: *Wer erschoss John F. Kennedy? Auf der Spur der Mörder von Dallas*
   Aus dem Amerikanischen von Uwe Anton. Bergisch Gladbach: Gustav Lübbe Verlag
   GmbH 1992 (Jim Garrison Original 1988).

Kläui, Jenny: *Maturaarbeit "John F. Kennedy – Profiles in Courage",* 2003

Zellweger, Kim: *Maturaarbeit "Das Attentat auf John F. Kennedy",* 2003

Films:
NTV-reportage in cooperation with BBC: *"Die Ermordung John F. Kennedy's",* 2005

Internet addresses:

http://www.hdg.de/lemo/html/biografien/KennedyJohnF/. April 3, 2006

http://history1900s.about.com/gi/dynamic/offsite.htm?zi=1/XJ&sdn=history1900s&zu=http%
3A%2F%2Fwww.biography.com%2Fsearch%2Farticle.jsp%3Faid%3D9362930%26search%
3D   April 3, 2006

http://www.swissdox.ch/cgi-bin/cqcgi_703_5/@rw_sd_set2_minus.de.env?CQ_SESS... April
4, 2006
Zeitungsartikel von swissdox:
   Tages-Anzeiger, 06.01.2006
   Blick; November 24, 1994

http://de.wikipedia.org/wiki/Attentat_auf_John_F._Kennedy April 4, 2006

http://historynet.com/ah/bl4days/index3.html July 15, 2006

http://en.wikipedia.org/wiki/Jfk_assassination July 19, 2006

http://en.wikipedia.org/wiki/Lee_Harvey_Oswald#Oswald.27s_flight_and_the_murder_of_Of ficer_J._D._Tippit July 19, 2006

http://icky.de/index2.htm July 19, 2006

http://en.wikipedia.org/wiki/Jim_Garrison July 21, 2006

http://en.wikipedia.org/wiki/Image:JFKmotorcade.jpg July 22, 2006

http://en.wikipedia.org/wiki/Image:Dealey-plaza-annotated.png July 22, 2006

http://en.wikipedia.org/wiki/Image:Oswald_shot_by_Ruby_%28Pulitzer%29.jpgJuly 22, 2006

http://www.wdr.de/tv/dokumentation/rendezvous_mit_dem_tod.phtml August 4, 2006

http://files.blog-city.com/files/A05/141484/p/f/young_castro_2.jpg August 4, 2006

http://en.wikipedia.org/wiki/Kennedy_assassination_theories#Two_shooters August 9, 2006

http://en.wikipedia.org/wiki/War_of_vietnam August 10, 2006

http://en.wikipedia.org/wiki/Lyndon_B._Johnson August 10, 2006 http://www.3sat.de/3sat.php?http://www.3sat.de/kulturzeit/themen/53102/index.html   August 10, 2006

http://mcadams.posc.mu.edu/route.htm   August 11, 2006

http://mcadams.posc.mu.edu/jimlie.htm   August 11, 2006

http://www.posner.com/articles/garrison.htm   August 11, 2006

http://verschwoerungen.info/wiki/John_F._Kennedy August 12, 2006

http://en.wikipedia.org/wiki/Oswald%27s_Tale   August 13, 2006